PLANT BASED COOKBOOK FOR BEGINNERS

By
Sandra Bloggs

TABLE OF CONTENTS

BREAKFAST

The Berry-Blend Bowl

Preparation time: 5 minutes
Cooking time: 0 minutes
Servings: 2

Ingredients:
2 cups unsweetened soy milk
1 cup frozen blueberries

- 1 cup frozen pitted cherries
- 2 bananas, sliced
- 1 cup Maple Muesli or granola
- 4 tablespoons hemp seeds

Directions:

1. In a blender, combine the soy milk, blueberries, and cherries and purée until smooth. Divide the purée between two serving bowls.
2. Arrange the banana slices halfway around the edge of each bowl. Spoon ½ cup of Maple Muesli into the center of each bowl.
3. Spoon 2 tablespoons of hemp seeds around the edge of each bowl, opposite the bananas, and serve.

Nutrition: Calories: 540Fat: 18gProtein: 17gCarbs: 84g

Breakfast Buddha Bowl

Preparation time: 15 minutes
Cooking time: 35 minutes
Servings: 4

Ingredients:
*   3 tablespoons rice vinegar
*   ½ cup diced yellow onion
*   2 carrots, diced
*   1 cup amaranth
*   1 cup rolled oats
*   4 cups tightly packed leafy greens (kale, spinach, or Swiss chard)
*   1 (15-ounce) can adzuki beans, drained and rinsed
*   ¼ cup nutritional yeast
*   2 tablespoons low-sodium soy sauce or tamari

Directions:
1. In a large saucepan, heat the vinegar over medium-high heat until bubbling. Add the onion and carrots and cook until the onion is translucent about 5 minutes.
2. Add the amaranth and 2½ cups water and boil; adjust the heat to low and simmer for 10 minutes. Add the oats, raise the heat to medium-high, and return to a gentle boil.
3. Add the leafy greens and adzuki beans and stir. Lower the heat to low and simmer until the mixture is thick and the oats are tender, 10 to 15 minutes more.

4. Remove from the heat and stir in the nutritional yeast and soy sauce, then serve.

Nutrition: Calories: 414 Fat: 5g Protein: 20g Carbs: 73g

Turmeric Tofu Scramble

Preparation time: 10 minutes
Cooking time: 15 minutes
Servings: 4

Ingredients:
- 2 tablespoons Vegetable Broth or water
- 1 cup diced yellow onion
- ½ cup diced carrot
- ½ cup diced celery
- 1 (14-ounce) block extra-firm tofu, pressed & drained
- 1 teaspoon ground turmeric
- ½ teaspoon smoked paprika
- ½ teaspoon chili powder
- 2 cups tightly packed chopped kale
- ½ teaspoon salt or Spicy Umami Blend

Directions:
1. Warm your broth on medium-high heat in a large skillet. Add the onion, carrot, and celery and sauté until the onion begins to soften about 3 minutes.
2. Crumble the tofu with your hands into the skillet. Add the turmeric, smoked paprika, and chili powder, stir well and cook for 5 minutes.
3. Add the kale and stir well. Cover the skillet, adjust the heat to medium-low, and cook for 5 minutes more. Stir in the salt and serve.

Nutrition: Calories: 123 Fat: 6g Protein: 11g Carbs: 9g,l

Tempeh "Sausage" Patties

Preparation time: 15 minutes
Cooking time: 20 minutes
Servings: 4

Ingredients:
- 8 ounces tempeh
- 2 tablespoons nutritional yeast
- 2 garlic cloves, minced
- ½ teaspoon smoked paprika
- ½ teaspoon fennel seed
- ¼ teaspoon anise seed
- ¼ teaspoon red pepper flakes
- ¼ teaspoon salt or Spicy Umami Blend
- ¼ teaspoon freshly ground black or white pepper
- Vegetable oil spray or 3 tablespoons aquafaba (optional)

Directions:
1. Warm oven to 400°F. Prepare your baking sheet lined using a parchment paper or a silicone baking mat.
2. Place a steamer basket or trivet in a large saucepan. Pour in 2 cups water and bring to a boil over high heat. Place the tempeh in the steamer basket or on the trivet, cover, lower the heat to medium, and steam for 5 minutes.
3. Using tongs, transfer the tempeh to a food processor and break it into four large pieces—pulse for a few seconds to break up the tempeh into large chunks.
4. Add the nutritional yeast, garlic, paprika, fennel, anise, red pepper flakes, salt, and pepper. Pulse in short bursts, adding 1 or 2 tablespoons water as needed, until thoroughly combined, with a chunky, dough-like texture.
5. Form the mixture into 4 patties about ½ inch thick and place them on the prepared baking sheet. Mist the top of the patties with vegetable oil or brush with aquafaba.
6. Bake for 8 minutes, then flip the patties, mist the tops with vegetable oil or brush with aquafaba, and bake for 8 minutes more.

Nutrition: Calories: 113 Fat: 6g Protein: 11g Carbs: 6g

Indian-Style Lentil and Potato Hash

Preparation time: 10 minutes
Cooking time: 15 minutes
Servings: 4

Ingredients:
- ¼ cup Vegetable Broth/water, plus more if needed
- 1 (10-ounce) russet potato, unpeeled, cut into ¼-inch pieces
- 1 teaspoon ground cumin
- ½ teaspoon ground allspice
- ½ teaspoon ground ginger
- ½ teaspoon garam masala
- ½ teaspoon salt or Spicy Umami Blend (optional)
- 1 (15-ounce) can brown lentils, drained and rinsed
- ½ cup chopped green onions
- ½ cup chopped fresh cilantro (optional)
- ¼ cup chopped peanuts (optional)

Directions:
1. Warm broth over medium-high heat in a large skillet. Add the potato, cumin, allspice, ginger, garam masala, and salt (if using) and cook, frequently stirring, until the potato is tender, about 10 minutes. Put more broth or water as needed to maintain a very thick sauce consistency.
2. Add the lentils and stir to combine. Adjust the heat to medium, cover, then cook for 5 minutes more.
3. Divide the lentil mixture among four bowls. Top each serving with 2 tablespoons of green onions, 2 tablespoons of cilantro, and 1 tablespoon of peanuts, then serve.

Nutrition: Calories: 148 Fat: 1g Protein: 8g Carbs: 29g

Maple Muesli

Preparation time: 30 minutes
Cooking time: 20 minutes
Servings: 5

Ingredients:
- ½ cup dry millet
- 2 cups rolled oats
- 1 cup chopped walnuts
- ½ cup pure maple syrup
- 1 cup chopped pitted dates

Directions:
1. Preheat the oven to 350°F. Prepare your baking sheet lined using a parchment paper or a silicone baking mat. Rinse the millet, drain, and shake off as much water as possible. Heat a medium skillet over medium-high heat.
2. Put the millet in the hot skillet and cook, frequently stirring, until it becomes dry and aromatic and begins to make popping noises, 5 to 8 minutes. Immediately transfer the millet to a large bowl and let cool for 10 minutes.
3. Add the oats, walnuts, and maple syrup and stir until well combined. Transfer the muesli to the prepared baking sheet and bake for 18 minutes.
4. Place the baking sheet on a wire rack and let cool. Stir in the dates, then transfer the muesli to an airtight container.

Nutrition: Calories: 515Fat: 18g Protein: 12g Carbs: 82g

Fruity Yogurt Parfait

Preparation time: 5 minutes
Cooking time: 0 minutes
Servings: 2

Ingredients:
- 2 cups plain plant-based yogurt or Cashew Cream
- 2 cups fresh blueberries or raspberries
- 1 cup Maple Muesli or granola
- ¼ teaspoon ground cinnamon

Directions:
1. In an individual serving bowl or parfait glass, layer ½ cup of yogurt, 1 cup of berries, ½ cup of muesli, another ½ cup of yogurt, and 1/8 teaspoon of cinnamon. Repeat in a second serving bowl or parfait glass.

Nutrition: Calories: 520 Fat: 30g Protein: 14g Carbs: 71g

Apple Avocado Toast

Preparation time: 5 minutes
Cooking time: 2 minutes
Servings: 4

Ingredients:
- 1 large ripe avocado, halved and pitted
- 1 small apple, cored
- 2 tablespoons lemon juice
- ½ cup chopped pecans
- ½ teaspoon ground cinnamon
- 4 slices whole-grain bread, toasted

Directions:
1. Scoop your avocado flesh into a small bowl, then mash it with a fork. Cut the apple into 1/8-inch cubes and add it to the avocado.
2. Add the lemon juice, pecans, and cinnamon and gently fold with a rubber spatula until well combined.
3. Spread about ¼ cup of the apple-avocado mixture onto each slice of toast and serve.

Nutrition: Calories: 276 Fat: 19g Protein: 7g Carbs: 25g

Granola Cereal

Preparation time: 15 minutes
Cooking time: 40 minutes
Servings: 10
Ingredients:

- 3 cups old-fashioned rolled oats
- 1/2 cup pecans, coarsely chopped
- 3/4 cup unsweetened shredded coconut
- 1/4 cup coconut sugar/brown sugar
- 1/2 teaspoon cinnamon
- 3/4 teaspoon sea salt
- 3/4 cup maple syrup
- 1 teaspoon vanilla extract
- 1 cup raisins

Directions:

1. Preheat oven to 300°F. Line 2 baking sheets with parchment paper.
2. Combine the oats, pecans, coconut, sugar, cinnamon, and salt in a large bowl.
3. Combine maple syrup plus vanilla extract in a separate bowl. Combine both mixtures and evenly spread onto baking sheets.
4. Cook within 35 to 40 minutes until golden brown, stirring every 15 minutes to achieve an even color.
5. Remove from oven and let cool. Transfer into a large bowl.
6. Add raisins and mix until well combined.
7. Store in an airtight container.

Nutrition: Calories 280Fat 8g Carbohydrate 51g Protein 4g

Banana Pancakes

Preparation time: 15 minutes
Cooking time: 20 minutes
Servings: 10

Ingredients:

- 1 cup whole wheat flour
- 1 teaspoon baking powder
- 1/2 teaspoon cinnamon
- 1/4 teaspoon sea salt
- 1 large ripe banana
- 1 cup almond milk
- 1/4 cup unsweetened applesauce
- 1/2 teaspoon apple cider vinegar
- 1 teaspoon vanilla extract

Directions:

1. Combine all dry fixings in a medium-size bowl.
2. Mash banana in a separate bowl.
3. Combine wet ingredients with the mashed banana.
4. Mix the dry fixings with the wet fixings until well combined. Heat a nonstick pan on medium.
5. Put a spoonful of the batter onto the pan and cook until bubbles begin to form.
6. Flip pancake and cook until golden color appears.
7. Repeat until all the batter is gone.
8. Drizzle with maple syrup and serve.

Nutrition: Calories 67 Fat 1g Carbohydrate 14g Protein 3g

Hash Brown Cakes

Preparation time: 15 minutes
Cooking time: 10 minutes
Servings: 4

Ingredients:

- 2 potatoes, peeled and grated
- 1/2 small onion, diced
- 1/4 cup whole wheat flour
- 1 tablespoon nutritional yeast
- 1/2 teaspoon sea salt
- Black pepper to taste

Directions:

1. Peel and coarsely shred potatoes using a grater or in a food processor.
2. Rinse with cold water in your colander, then drain well and then pat dry with paper towels.
3. Place potatoes in a large bowl.
4. Stir in the onions, flour, nutritional yeast, salt, and pepper.
5. Mix well—Preheat a large nonstick skillet over medium heat.
6. For each cake, scoop 1/4 of the potato mixture onto the skillet. Press down the potato batter with a spatula to flatten evenly—Cook within 5 minutes.
7. Using a wide spatula, carefully turn potato cakes.
8. Cook again within 3 to 5 minutes more or until golden brown.

Nutrition: Calories 110Fat 0gCarbohydrate 24gProtein 4g

LUNCH

Falafel Kale Salad with Tahini Dressing

Preparation time: 15 minutes
Cooking time: 0 minutes
Servings: 4

Ingredients:
- 12 balls Vegan Falafels
- 6 cups kale, chopped
- 1/2 red onion, thinly sliced

- 2 slices pita bread, cut in squares
- 1 jalapeño, chopped
- Tahini Dressing
- 1-2 lemons, juiced

Directions:

1. In a mixing bowl, combine kale and lemon juice and toss well to mix. Place into the refrigerator.
2. Divide kale among four bowls.
3. Top with three Falafel balls, red onion, jalapeño and pita slices.
4. Top with tahini dressing and serve.

Nutrition: Calories 178Fat 2.8 g Carbs 16 g Protein 4 g

Fig and Kale Salad

Preparation time: 15 minutes
Cooking time: 0 minutes
Servings: 2

Ingredients:

- 1 ripe avocado
- 2 tablespoons lemon juice
- 3 ½ oz kale, packed, stems removed and cut into large sized bits
- 1 carrot, shredded
- 1 yellow zucchini, diced
- 4 fresh figs
- ¼ cup ground flaxseed
- 1 cup mixed green leaves
- 1 teaspoon sea salt

Directions:

1. Add kale to a bowl with avocado, lemon juice and sea salt.
2. Massage together until kale wilts.
3. Add in zucchini, carrot and 2 cups mixed green leaves.
4. Fold in figs and remaining ingredients.
5. Toss and serve.

Nutrition: Calories 255Fat 12.5 g Carbs 35 g Protein 6 g

Cucumber Avocado Toast

Preparation time: 15 minutes
Cooking time: 0 minutes
Servings: 2
Ingredients:

- 1 cucumber, sliced
- 2 sprouted (essene) bread slices, toasted
- ¼ handful basil leaves, chopped
- 4 tablespoons avocado, mashed
- Salt and pepper, to taste
- 1 teaspoon lemon juice

Directions:

1. Combine lemon juice together with the mashed avocado, and then spread the mixture on two bread slices.
2. Top with cucumber slices along with the finely chopped basil leaves. Generously sprinkle with salt and pepper and enjoy!

Nutrition: Calories 232Fat 14 g Carbs 24 g Protein 5 g

Kale and Cucumber Salad

Preparation time: 15 minutes
Cooking time: 50 minutes
Servings: 2

Ingredients:

- 1 garlic clove
- 3 ½ oz fresh ginger
- 1/2 green Thai chili
- 1 ½ tablespoons sugar
- 1 ½ tablespoons fish sauce
- 1 ½ tablespoons vegetable oil
- 1 English cucumber, thinly sliced

- 1 bunch red Russian kale, ribs and stems removed; leaves torn into small pieces
- 1 Persian cucumber, thinly sliced
- 2 tablespoons fresh lime juice
- 1 small red onion, sliced
- 1 teaspoon sugar
- 2 tablespoons cilantro, chopped
- Salt, to taste

Directions:

1. Heat the broiler and broil ginger, with skin for 50 minutes, turning once.
2. Let cool and slice.
3. Blend chili, ginger, garlic, sugar, fish sauce, oil and 2 tablespoon water in a blender until paste forms.
4. Toss ¼ cup dressing and kale in a bowl and coat well. Massage with hands until kale softens.
5. Toss Persian and English cucumbers, lime juice, onion and sugar in a bowl and season with salt.
6. Let it sit for 10 minutes.
7. Add the cucumber mixture to the bowl with kale and toss to combine.
8. Top with cilantro and serve.

Nutrition: Calories 160Fat 8 g Carbs 22 g Protein 3 g

Mexican Quinoa

Preparation time: 15 minutes
Cooking time: 8 minutes
Servings: 4

Ingredients:

- 1 cup quinoa, uncooked and rinsed
- 1 ½ cup vegetable broth
- 3 cups diced tomatoes
- 2 cups frozen corn
- 1 cup fresh parsley, chopped

- 1 onion, chopped
- 3 cloves of garlic, minced
- 2 bell peppers, chopped
- 1 tablespoon paprika powder
- ½ tablespoon cumin
- 2 tablespoons olive oil
- 2 tablespoons lime juice
- 2 green onions, chopped
- salt and pepper

Directions:
1. Place a large pot over medium heat.
2. Add olive oil.
3. Cook onions for 3 minutes.
4. Add garlic, bell peppers and cook for 5 minutes.
5. Add the remaining ingredients except for lime juice, green onions and parsley.
6. Cover and cook for about 20 minutes, keep checking to make sure the quinoa doesn't stick and burn.
7. Add lime juice, green onions and parsley.
8. Season the dish with salt and pepper before serving.

Nutrition: Calories 231Fat 17.8 g Carbs 19 g Protein 2 g

Mediterranean Parsley Salad

Preparation time: 15 minutes
Cooking time: 0 minutes
Servings: 2

Ingredients:
- ½ red onion, thinly sliced
- 1 cups parsley, chopped
- 1 Roma tomato, seeded and diced
- 6 mints, chopped
- 3 tablespoons currants, died
- 1 green chili, minced
- 1 tablespoon lemon

- 2 tablespoons olive oil
- 1/8 teaspoon sumac
- 1/8 teaspoon pepper, cracked
- ¼ teaspoon salt

Directions:
1. Mix lemon juice, olive oil, sumac, salt and pepper in a bowl and whisk to combine well.
2. Toss parsley with the remaining ingredients in a separate bowl.
3. Add the olive oil mixture to it and toss well and serve.

Nutrition: Calories 110Fat 8 g Carbs 7 g Protein 1 g

Tomatoes Parsley Salad

Preparation time: 15 minutes
Cooking time: 0 minutes
Servings: 2

Ingredients:
- 2 cups curly parsley leaves, packed
- 1 teaspoon garlic, minced
- 3/4 cup oil-packed sundried tomatoes, drained and julienned
- 2 tablespoons olive oil
- ½ cup basil leaves
- 2 tablespoons rice vinegar
- 1 shallot, minced
- 1 garlic clove, minced
- Salt and black pepper, to taste

Directions:
1. Wash parsley, dry and add to a bowl.
2. Add garlic and tomatoes.
3. Toss well.
4. Wash basil and dry it.
5. Add it to a blender and add vinegar, oil, salt and pepper to it.
6. Blend until smooth.

7. Add garlic and shallots to the dressing.
8. Add the dressing over salad and toss well.
9. Divide among 6 salad plates and serve.

Nutrition: Calories 245Fat 19.8 g Carbs 12 g Protein 7 g

Pumpkin and Brussels Sprouts Mix

Preparation time: 15 minutes
Cooking time: 35-40 minutes
Servings: 8

Ingredients:
- 1 lb. Brussels sprouts, halved
- 1 pumpkin, peeled, cubed
- 4 garlic cloves, sliced
- 2 tablespoons fresh parsley, chopped
- 2 tablespoons balsamic vinegar
- 1/3 cup olive oil
- Salt, pepper, to taste

Directions:
1. Warm oven to 400 degrees F. Prepare a baking dish and coat with cooking spray.
2. Mix sprouts, pumpkin and garlic in a bowl.
3. Add oil and toss well to coat the vegetables.
4. Transfer to the baking dish and cook for 35-40 minutes.
5. Stir once halfway.
6. Serve topped with parsley.

Nutrition: Calories 152Fat 9 g Carbohydrate 17 g Protein 4 g

Strawberry Spinach Salad

Preparation time: 15 minutes
Cooking time: 0 minutes
Servings: 4

Ingredients:
- 5 cups baby spinach
- 2 cups strawberries, sliced
- 2 tablespoons lemon juice
- 1/2 teaspoon Dijon mustard
- 1/4 cup olive oil
- 3/4 cup toasted almonds, chopped
- 1/4 red onion, sliced
- Salt, pepper, to taste

Directions:
1. Take a large bowl and mix Dijon mustard with lemon juice in it, and slowly add olive oil and combine.
2. Season the mixture with black pepper and salt.
3. Now, mix strawberries, half cup of almonds, and sliced onion in a bowl.
4. Pour the dressing on top and toss to combine.
5. Serve the salad topped with almonds and vegan cheese.

Nutrition: Calories 116Fat 3 g Carbs 13 g Protein 6 g

Kale Power Salad

Preparation time: 15 minutes
Cooking time: 40 minutes
Servings: 2

Ingredients:
- 1 bunch kale, ribs removed and chopped
- 1/2 cup quinoa
- 1 tablespoon olive oil
- 1/2 lime, juiced
- ½ teaspoon salt
- 1 tablespoon olive oil
- 1 red rose potato, cut into small cubes
- 1 teaspoon ground cumin
- 3/4 teaspoons salt

- 1/2 teaspoon smoked paprika
- 1 lime, juiced
- 1 avocado, sliced into long strips
- 1 tablespoon olive oil
- 1 tablespoon cilantro leaves
- 1 jalapeno, deseeded, membranes removed and chopped
- salt
- ¼ cup pepitas

Directions:

1. Rinse quinoa in a running water for 2 minutes. Mix 2 cups water and rinsed quinoa in a pot, reduce heat to simmer and cook for 15 minutes.
2. Remove quinoa from heat and let rest, covered, for 5 minutes. Uncover pot, drain excess water and fluff quinoa with a fork. Let cool.
3. Warm-up olive oil in a pan over medium heat. Add chopped red rose potatoes and toss. Add smoked paprika, cumin and salt. Mix to combine.
4. Add ¼ cup water once pan is sizzling. Cover the pan then adjust heat to low. Cook for 10 minutes, stirring occasionally. Uncover pan, raise heat to medium and cook for 7 minutes. Set aside to cool.
5. Transfer kale to a bowl and add salt to it and massage with hands. Scrunch handfuls of kale in your hands. Repeat until kale is darker in color.
6. Mix 2 tablespoons olive oil, ½ teaspoon salt and 1 lime juice in a bowl. Add over the kale and toss to coat.
7. Add 2 avocados, 2 lime juices, 2 tablespoons olive oil, jalapeno, cilantro leaves and salt in a blender. Blend well and season the avocado sauce.
8. Toast pepitas in a skillet over medium low heat for 5 minutes, stirring frequently. Add quinoa to the kale bowl and toss to combine well.
9. Divide kale and quinoa mixture into 4 bowls. Top with red rose potatoes, avocado sauce, and pepitas. Enjoy!

Nutrition: Calories 250Fat 11 g Carbs 25 g Protein 9 g

Apple Spinach Salad

Preparation time: 15 minutes
Cooking time: 0 minutes
Servings: 4

Ingredients:
- 5 ounces fresh spinach
- 1/4 red onion, sliced
- 1 apple, sliced
- 1/4 cup sliced toasted almonds
- For the Dressing:
- 3 tablespoons red wine vinegar
- 1/3 cup olive oil
- 1 minced garlic clove
- 2 teaspoons Dijon mustard
- Salt, pepper, to taste

Directions:
1. Combine red wine vinegar, olive oil, garlic, and Dijon mustard in a bowl. Season with black pepper and salt.
2. In a separate bowl mix fresh spinach, apple, onion, toasted almonds. Pour the dressing on top and toss to combine.
3. Serve

Nutrition: Calories 232Fat 20.8 g Carbs 10 g Protein 3 g

DINNER

Mint and Berry Soup

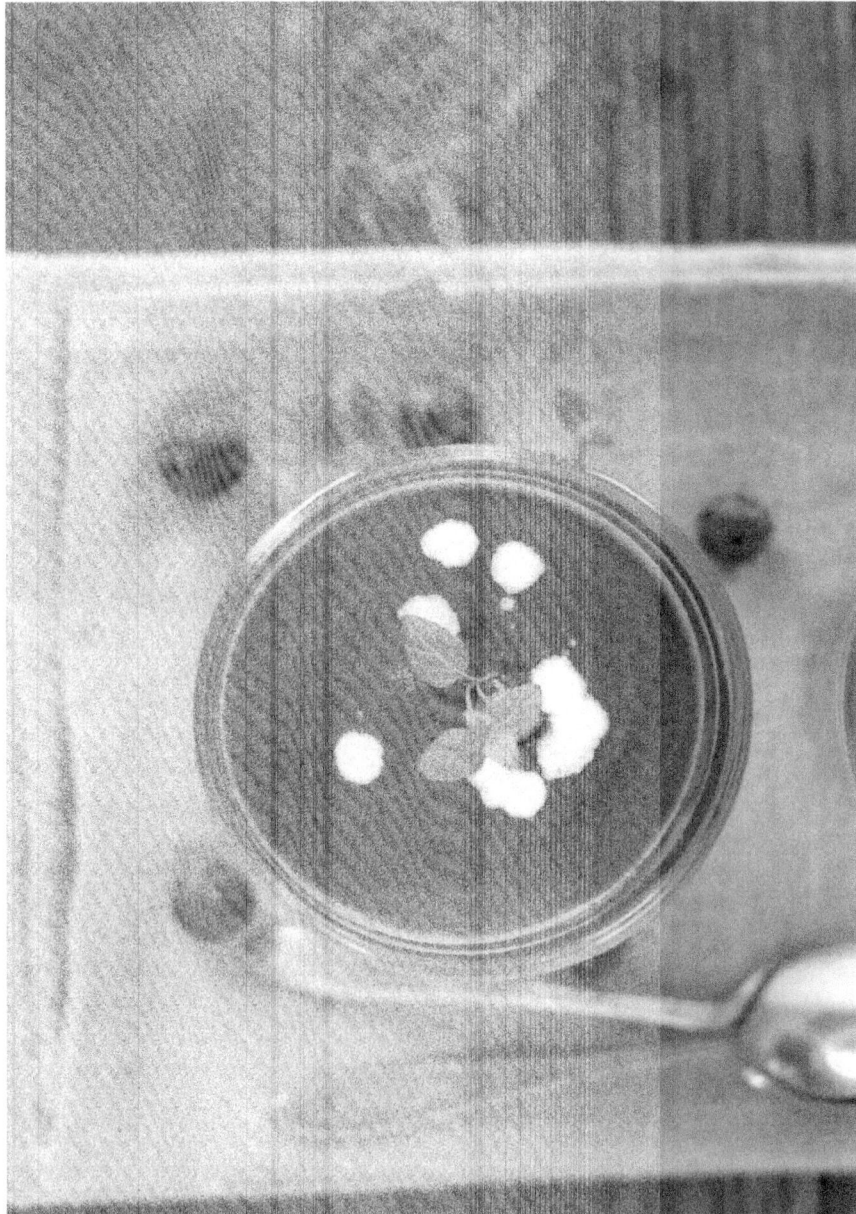

Preparation time: 35 minutes
Cooking time: 0 minutes
Servings: 1

Ingredients:
Sweetener:
- ¼ cup Water, plus more if needed
- ¼ cup Unrefined whole cane sugar

Soup:
- ½ cup water
- 1 cup mixed berries
- 8 mint leaves
- 1 tsp lemon juice

Directions:
1. Put the water and sugar to a small pot and cook, stirring constantly, until the sugar has dissolved. Allow this to cool.
2. Add the mint leaves, lemon juice, water, berries, and the cooled sugar mixture to a blender. Mix everything together until smooth.
3. Pour into a basin then put in the refrigerator till the broth is completely chilled. This will take about 20 minutes. Enjoy.

Nutrition: Calories: 240 Carbs: 14g Fat: 17gProtein: 6g

Mushroom Soup

Preparation time: 15 minutes
Cooking time: 10 minutes
Servings: 2

Ingredients:
- 13 ½ oz Full-fat coconut milk
- 1 cup Vegetable broth
- ½ tsp Pepper
- ¾ tsp Sea salt
- 1 Crush garlic clove
- 1 cup Diced onion

- 1 cup Cut up cremini mushrooms
- 1 cup Cut up Chinese black mushrooms
- 1 tbsp Avocado oil
- 1 tbsp Coconut aminos
- ½ tsp Dried thyme

Directions:

1. Warm up the grease in a very massive pan then put in all the seasonings: pepper, salt, garlic, onion bulb, and mushrooms.
2. Boil and prepare everything along for a few minutes, either that or till the onions turn soft.
3. Mix in the coconut aminos, thyme, coconut milk, and vegetable broth.
4. Lower the fire down then allow the broth to boil on approximately a quarter-hour.
5. Mix the broth from time to time.
6. Taste and adjust any of the seasonings that you need to.
7. Divide into two bowls and enjoy.

Nutrition: Calories: 129 Carbs: 4g Fat: 10g Protein: 2g

Potato Lentil Stew

Preparation time: 15 minutes
Cooking time: 30 minutes
Servings: 4

Ingredients:

- 2 sprigs chopped oregano sprigs
- diced celery stalk
- 1 cup cubed and peeled potato
- 2 sliced carrots
- 1 cup dry lentils
- 1 tsp spicy condiment / pepper,
- 1 to 1 ½ tsp seawater salt
- 2 mashed garlic bulbs
- ½ cup diced onion

- 2 tbsp avocado oil
- 13 ½ oz full-fat coconut milk
- 5 cups vegetable broth, divided
- 2 sprigs chopped tarragon

Directions:

1. Using a big cooking utensil, warm the avocado grease together with putting in seasonings: pepper, salt, garlic bulbs, together with onion. Cook within 3 to 5 minutes, or until the onion has become soft.
2. Mix in the tarragon, oregano, celery, potato, carrots, lentils, and 2 ½ cups of the vegetable broth.
3. Mix everything together.
4. Enable the casserole to return up to heat and then lower the fire down.
5. Let this cook, stirring often.
6. Add in extra vegetable broth in half cup portions as needed.
7. Let the stew cook for 20 to 25 minutes, or until the lentils and potatoes are soft. Set the stew off the heat and mix in the coconut milk.
8. Divide into four bowls and enjoy.

Nutrition: Calories: 240 Carbs: 14g Fat: 17gProtein: 6g

Beans Curry

Preparation time: 10 minutes
Cooking time: 8 hours and 10 minutes
Servings: 5

Ingredients:

- 2 cups kidney beans, dried, soaked
- 1-inch of ginger, grated
- 1 ½ cup diced tomatoes
- 1 medium red onion, peeled, sliced
- 1 tablespoon tomato paste
- 1 teaspoon minced garlic
- 1 small bunch cilantro, chopped

- ½ teaspoon cumin powder
- 1 teaspoon salt
- 1 ½ teaspoon curry powder
- 2 tablespoons olive oil
- 2 tablespoons lemon juice

Directions:

1. Place onion in a food processor, add ginger and garlic, and pulse for 1 minute until blended.
2. Take a skillet pan, place it over medium heat, add oil and when hot, add the onion-garlic mixture, and cook for 5 minutes until softened and light brown.
3. Then add tomatoes and tomato paste, stir in ½ teaspoon salt, cumin and curry powder and cook for 5 minutes until cooked.
4. Drain the soaked beans, add them to the slow cooker, add cooked tomato mixture, and remaining ingredients except for cilantro and lemon juice and stir until mixed.
5. Switch on the slow cooker, then shut with lid and cook for 8 hours at high heat setting until tender.
6. When done, transfer 1 cup of beans to the blender, process until creamy, then return it into the slow cooker and stir until mixed. Drizzle with lemon juice, top with cilantro, and serve.

Nutrition: Calories: 252 Fat: 6.5 g Carbs: 38 g Protein: 13 g

Pasta with Kidney Bean Sauce

Preparation time: 5 minutes
Cooking time: 15 minutes
Servings: 4

Ingredients:

- 12 ounces cooked kidney beans
- 7 ounces whole-wheat pasta, cooked
- 1 medium white onion, peeled, diced
- 1 cup arugula

- 2 tablespoons tomato paste
- 1 teaspoon minced garlic
- ½ teaspoon smoked paprika
- 1 teaspoon dried oregano
- ½ teaspoon cayenne pepper
- 1/3 teaspoon ground black pepper
- 2/3 teaspoon salt
- 2 tablespoons balsamic vinegar

Directions:
1. Take a large skillet pan, place it over medium-high heat, add onion and garlic, splash with some water and cook for 5 minutes.
2. Then add remaining ingredients, except for pasta and arugula, stir until mixed and cook for 10 minutes until thickened.
3. When done, mash with the fork, top with arugula and serve with pasta. Serve straight away.

Nutrition: Calories: 236 Fat: 1.6 g Carbs: 46 g Protein: 12 g

Broccoli and Rice Stir Fry

Preparation time: 5 minutes
Cooking time: 10 minutes
Servings: 8

Ingredients:
- 16 ounces frozen broccoli florets, thawed
- 3 green onions, diced
- ½ teaspoon salt
- ¼ teaspoon ground black pepper
- 2 tablespoons soy sauce
- 1 tablespoon olive oil
- 1 ½ cups white rice, cooked

Directions:

1. Take a skillet pan, place it over medium heat, add broccoli, and cook for 5 minutes until tender-crisp.
2. Then add scallion and other ingredients, toss until well mixed and cook for 2 minutes until hot. Serve straight away.

Nutrition: Calories: 187 Fat: 3.4 g Carbs: 33 g Protein: 6.3 g

<u>Lentil, Rice and Vegetable Bake</u>

Preparation time: 10 minutes
Cooking time: 40 minutes
Servings: 6

Ingredients:
- 1/2 cup white rice, cooked
- 1 cup red lentils, cooked
- 1/3 cup chopped carrots
- 1 medium tomato, chopped
- 1 small onion, peeled, chopped
- 1/3 cup chopped zucchini
- 1/3 cup chopped celery
- 1 ½ teaspoon minced garlic
- ½ teaspoon ground black pepper
- 1 teaspoon dried basil
- 1 teaspoon ground cumin
- 1 teaspoon dried oregano
- ½ teaspoon salt
- 1 teaspoon olive oil
- 8 ounces tomato sauce

Directions:
1. Take a skillet pan, place it over medium heat, add oil and when hot, add onion and garlic, and cook for 5 minutes.
2. Then add remaining vegetables, season with salt, black pepper, and half of each cumin, oregano and basil and cook for 5 minutes until vegetables are tender.
3. Take a casserole dish, place lentils and rice in it, top with vegetables, spread with tomato sauce and sprinkle with

remaining cumin, oregano, and basil, and bake for 30 minutes until bubbly. Serve straight away.

Nutrition: Calories: 187 Fat: 1.5 g Carbs: 35.1 g Protein: 9.7 g

Corn and Potato Chowder

Preparation time: 5 minutes
Cooking time: 35 minutes
Servings: 4

Ingredients:
- 2 ears of corn
- 10 ounces tofu, extra-firm, drained cubed
- 1 1/2 cups frozen corn kernels
- 1/4 medium onion, peeled, chopped
- 3 medium potatoes, peeled, cubed
- 1/4 medium red bell pepper, cored, chopped
- ¼ cup cilantro, chopped
- 2/3 teaspoon salt
- 1/4 cup coconut cream
- 7 cups of vegetable broth

Directions:
1. Prepare the ears of corn and for this, remove their skin and husk, then cut each corn into four pieces and place them in a large pot.
2. Place the pot over medium-high heat, add cilantro, onion and bell pepper, pour in the broth, bring the mixture to boil, then switch heat to medium level and cook for 20 minutes until corn pieces are tender.
3. Add potatoes, cook for 8 minutes until fork tender, then add tofu and kernels, simmer for 5 minutes and taste to adjust seasoning.
4. Remove pot from heat, stir in cream until combined and serve straight away.

Nutrition: Calories: 159 Fat: 2.4 g Carbs: 29 g Protein: 6.6 g

Cauliflower Soup

Preparation time: 10 minutes
Cooking time: 40 minutes
Servings: 2

Ingredients:
- 1 small head of cauliflower, slice into florets
- 4 tablespoons pomegranate seeds
- 2 sprigs of thyme and more for garnishing
- 1 teaspoon minced garlic
- 2/3 teaspoon salt
- 1/3 teaspoon ground black pepper
- 1 tablespoon olive oil
- 1 1/2 cups vegetable stock
- 1/2 cup coconut milk, unsweetened

Directions:
1. Take a pot, place it over medium heat, add oil and when hot, add garlic and cook for 1 minute until fragrant.
2. Add florets, thyme, pour in the stock and bring the mixture to boil.
3. Switch heat to the medium low level, simmer the soup for 30 minutes until florets are tender, then remove the pot from heat, discard the thyme and puree using an immersion blender until smooth.
4. Stir milk into the soup, season with salt and black pepper, then garnish with pomegranate seeds and thyme sprigs and serve.

Nutrition: Calories: 184 Fat: 11 g Carbs: 17 g Protein: 3 g

Red Pepper and Tomato Soup

Preparation time: 10 minutes
Cooking time: 40 minutes
Servings: 4

Ingredients:

- 2 carrots, peeled, chopped
- 1 1/4 pounds red bell peppers, deseeded, sliced into quarters
- 1/2 of medium red onion, peeled, sliced into thin wedges
- 16 ounces small tomatoes, halved
- 1 tablespoon chopped basil
- 1/2 teaspoon salt
- 2 cups vegetable broth

Directions:

1. Switch on the oven, then set it to 450 F and let it preheat. Then place all the vegetables in a single on a baking sheet lined with foil and roast for 40 minutes until the skins of peppers are slightly charred.
2. When done, remove the baking sheet from the oven, let them cool for 10 minutes, then peel the peppers and transfer all the vegetables into a blender.
3. Add basil and salt to the vegetables, pour in the broth, and puree the vegetables until smooth.
4. Serve straight away.

Nutrition: Calories: 77.4 Fat: 1.8 g Carbs: 14.4 g Protein: 3.3 g

SNACKS

Mushroom Dip

Preparation time: 10 minutes
Cooking time: 20 minutes
Servings: 4

Ingredients:
- ¼ cup coconut cream
- 1 teaspoon garlic powder
- 1 teaspoon chili powder
- 1 tablespoon olive oil
- 1 teaspoon oregano, dried
- 1 small yellow onion, chopped
- 24 ounces white mushroom caps
- Salt and black pepper to the taste
- 1 teaspoon curry powder

Directions:
1. Heat-up a pan with the oil over medium heat, add the onion, oregano, chili, curry and garlic and cook for 5 minutes.
2. Add the mushrooms and cook for 5 minutes more.

3. Add the rest of the ingredients, cook the mix for 10 minutes, cool down a bit, blend with an immersion blender and serve as a party dip.

Nutrition: Calories 224 Fat 11.4g Carbs 7g Protein 11g

Mango Salsa

Preparation time: 10 minutes
Cooking time: 0 minutes
Servings: 4

Ingredients:
- 2 cups cubed mango
- ¼ cup chopped chives
- 1 teaspoon mint, dried
- 1 teaspoon coriander, ground
- 1 tablespoon cilantro, chopped
- ½ cup red bell pepper, minced
- ½ cup chopped red onion
- 2 tablespoons olive oil
- Salt and black pepper to the taste
- Juice of 1 lime
- A pinch of red pepper flakes

Directions:
1. In a bowl, mix the mango with the chives, mint and the other ingredients, toss and serve.

Nutrition: Calories 100 Fat 3g Carbs 8g Protein 9g

Kale Bowls

Preparation time: 10 minutes
Cooking time: 10 minutes

Servings: 4

Ingredients:
- 2 tablespoons almonds, chopped
- 2 tablespoons walnuts, chopped
- 2 bunches kale, trimmed and roughly chopped
- 1 cup cherry tomatoes, halved
- Salt and black pepper to the taste
- 2 tablespoons avocado oil
- Juice of 1 lemon
- 2/3 cup jarred roasted peppers
- 1 teaspoon Italian seasoning
- ¼ teaspoon chili powder

Directions:
1. Warm-up a pan with the oil over medium heat, add kale and cook for 5 minutes.
2. Add the rest of the ingredients, toss, cook for 5 minutes more, divide into bowls and serve.

Nutrition: Calories 143 Fat 5.9g Carbs 9g Protein 7g

Green Bean Fries

Preparation time: 10 minutes
Cooking time: 8 hours
Servings: 8

Ingredients:
- 1/3 cup avocado oil
- 5 pounds green beans, trimmed
- Salt and black pepper to taste
- 1 teaspoon garlic powder
- 1 teaspoon onion powder
- 1 teaspoon turmeric powder
- 1 teaspoon oregano, dried
- 1 teaspoon mint, dried

Directions:

1. Mix the green beans with the oil, salt, pepper and the other ingredients in a bowl and toss well.
2. Put the green beans in your dehydrator and dry them for 8 hours at 135 degrees.

3. Serve cold as a snack.

Nutrition: Calories 100 Fat 12g Carbs 8g Protein 5g

Avocado Dip

Preparation time: 10 minutes
Cooking time: 0 minutes
Servings: 4

Ingredients:
- 2 avocados, peeled, pitted, chopped
- Salt and black pepper to the taste
- 1 tablespoon olive oil
- 1 teaspoon mint, dried
- 1 teaspoon curry powder
- 1 tablespoon green curry paste
- 4 garlic cloves, chopped
- ½ cup tahini
- 2 tablespoons lemon juice

Directions:
1. In a blender, mix the avocado with salt, pepper, the oil and the other ingredients. Pulse until smooth then divide into bowls and serve as a snack.

Nutrition: Calories 200 Fat 6.3g Carbs 9g Protein 7.6g

Vegan Eggplant Patties

Preparation time: 30 minutes
Cooking time: 15 minutes
Servings: 6

Ingredients

- 2 big eggplants
- 1 onion finely diced
- 1 tbsp smashed garlic cloves
- 1 bunch raw parsley, chopped
- 1/2 cup almond meal
- 4 tbsp kalamata olives, pitted and sliced
- 1 tbsp baking soda
- salt and ground pepper to taste
- olive oil or avocado oil, for frying

Directions

1. Peel off eggplants, rinse, and cut in half. Sauté eggplant cubes in a non-stick skillet - occasionally stirring - about 10 minutes.
2. Transfer to a large bowl and mash with an immersion blender. Add eggplant puree into a bowl and add in all remaining ingredients (except oil).
3. Knead a mixture using your hands until the dough is smooth, sticky, and easy to shape. Shape mixture into 6 patties.
4. Heat-up the olive oil in a frying skillet on medium-high heat. Fry patties for about 3 to 4 minutes per side. Remove patties on a platter lined with kitchen paper towel to drain. Serve warm.

Nutrition: Calories: 210 Carbs: 16g Fat: 12g Protein: 8g

Spinach Chips

Preparation time: 10 minutes
Cooking time: 20 minutes
Servings: 4

Ingredients:

- 1 pound baby spinach, well dried
- Salt and black pepper to the taste
- ½ teaspoon oregano, dried

- 1 teaspoon sweet paprika
- Cooking spray

Directions:
1. Oiled a baking sheet using cooking spray and spread the spinach leaves on it.
2. Add the other ingredients, toss gently and bake at 435 degrees F for 20 minutes.
3. Serve as a snack.

Nutrition: Calories 140 Fat 4.2g Carbs 6g Protein 4g

Balsamic Zucchini Bowls

Preparation time: 10 minutes
Cooking time: 3 hours
Servings: 8

Ingredients:
- 3 zucchinis, thinly sliced
- Salt and black pepper to the taste
- 2 tablespoons olive oil
- 1 teaspoon turmeric powder
- 1 teaspoon coriander, ground
- 2 tablespoons balsamic vinegar

Directions:
1. Spread the zucchini on a lined baking sheet and mix with the other ingredients.
2. Toss and bake at 360 degrees F for 3 hours.
3. Divide into bowls and serve as a snack.

Nutrition: Calories 100 Fat 3g Carbs 3g Protein 4.5g

VEGETABLES

Fried Rice and Vegetables

Preparation Time: 5 Minutes
Cooking Time: 25 Minutes
Serving: 4

Ingredients:
- 3/4 cup uncooked short- or long-grain white rice
- 1 1/2 cups water

- 2 tablespoons sesame oil, divided
- 2 large eggs, lightly beaten
- 2 carrots, diced
- 4 ounces (11/4 cups) sliced white mushrooms
- 1 tablespoon minced garlic
- 6 green onions, white and green parts, sliced and divided
- 2 tablespoons tamari or soy sauce
- 1/2 cup frozen green peas, defrosted

Directions:

1. Rinse the rice and add to a small saucepan.
2. Add the water and bring to a boil.
3. Reduce the heat to low, cover, and simmer for 15 minutes, until the water is absorbed.
4. Fluff with a fork and set aside.
5. While the rice is cooking, heat 1/2 tablespoon of the sesame oil in a large saucepan or wok over medium heat.
6. Add the eggs and cook without stirring for 5 minutes, until the egg is dry.
7. Remove to a plate and cut into small strips. Set aside.
8. Return the saucepan or wok to the heat.
9. Heat the remaining 2 1/2 tablespoons of sesame oil.
10. Add the carrots and stir for 2 minutes.
11. Add the mushrooms, garlic, and the white parts of the green onions. Stir for 3 more minutes.
12. Add the cooked rice and tamari or soy sauce.
13. Cook, stirring frequently, for 10 minutes, until the rice is sticky.
14. Toss in the green parts of the green onions, peas, and egg and stir to mix.
15. Remove from the heat and serve hot with extra tamari or soy sauce, if desired.

Nutrition: Calories: 271Total Fat: 10g Total Carbs: 37g Fiber:3g Sugar: 4gProtein: 9g Sodium: 567mg

Spanish-Style Saffron Rice with Black Beans

Preparation Time: 5 Minutes
Cooking Time: 25 Minutes
Serving: 4

Ingredients:
2 cups vegetable stock
1/4 teaspoon saffron threads (optional)
1 1/2 tablespoons extra-virgin olive oil
1 small red or yellow onion, halved and thinly sliced
1 tablespoon minced garlic
1 teaspoon turmeric
2 teaspoons paprika
1 cup long-grain white rice, well-rinsed
1 (14-ounce) can black beans, drained and rinsed
1/2 cup green beans, halved or quartered
1 small red bell pepper, chopped
1 teaspoon salt

Directions:
In a small pot, heat the vegetable stock until boiling. Add the saffron, if using, and remove from the heat.
Meanwhile, heat the olive oil in a large nonstick skillet over medium heat.
Add the onion, garlic, turmeric, paprika, and rice and stir to coat.
Pour in the stock, and mix in the black beans, green beans, and red bell pepper.
Bring to a boil, reduce the heat to medium-low, cover, and simmer until the rice is tender and most of the liquid has been absorbed, about 20 minutes.
Stir in the salt and serve hot.

Nutrition: Calories: 332 Total Fat: 5g Total Carbs: 63g Fiber: 9g Sugar: 2g Protein: 11g Sodium: 658mg

Pinto and Green Bean Fry with Couscous

Preparation Time: 5 Minutes
Cooking Time: 15 Minutes
Serving: 4

Ingredients:
- 1/2 cup water
- 1/3 cup couscous (semolina or whole-wheat)
- 2 tablespoons extra-virgin olive oil
- 1 small onion, chopped
- 1/2 tablespoon minced garlic
- 1 cup green beans, cut into 1-inch pieces
- 1 cup fresh or frozen corn
- 11/2 teaspoons chili powder
- 1/2 teaspoon ground cumin
- 1 large tomato, finely chopped
- 1 (14-ounce) can pinto beans, drained and rinsed
- 1 teaspoon salt

Directions:
1. Bring the water to a boil in a small saucepan. Remove from the heat and stir in the couscous. Cover the pan and let sit for 10 minutes.
2. Gently fluff the couscous with a fork.
3. While the couscous is cooking, heat the olive oil in a large skillet over medium heat. Add the onion and garlic and stir for 1 minute.
4. Add the green beans and stir for 4 minutes, until they begin to soften.
5. Add the corn, stir for another 2 minutes, then add the chili powder and cumin, and stir to coat the vegetables.
6. Add the tomato and simmer for 3 or 4 minutes. Stir in the pinto beans and couscous and cook for 3 to 4 minutes, until everything is heated throughout. Stir often.
7. Stir in the salt and serve hot or warm.

Nutrition: Calories: 267Total Fat: 8gTotal Carbs: 41g Fiber: 10g Sugar: 4 g Protein: 10g Sodium: 601mg

SALAD

Egg Avocado Salad

Preparation Time: 10 minutes
Cooking Time: 0 minute
Servings: 4

Ingredients:
- 1 avocado
- 6 hard-boiled eggs, peeled and chopped
- 1 tablespoon mayonnaise
- 2 tablespoons freshly squeezed lemon juice
- ¼ cup celery, chopped
- 2 tablespoons chives, chopped
- Salt and pepper to taste

Instructions:
1. Add the avocado to a large bowl.
2. Mash the avocado using a fork.
3. Stir in the egg and mash the eggs.
4. Add the mayo, lemon juice, celery, chives, salt and pepper.

5. Chill in the refrigerator for at least 30 minutes before serving.

Nutrition: Calories 224 Fat 18 g Saturated fat 3.9 Carbohydrates 6.1 g Fiber 3.6 g Protein 10.6 g

Pepper Tomato Salad

Preparation Time: 1 hour and 25 minutes
Cooking Time: 0 minute
Servings: 8

Ingredients:
- 2 tablespoons balsamic vinegar
- 2 tablespoons olive oil
- ½ teaspoon Dijon mustard
- 2 teaspoons fresh basil leaves, chopped
- 1 tablespoon fresh chives, chopped
- 1 teaspoon sugar
- Pepper to taste
- 2 cups yellow bell peppers, sliced into rings
- 1 cups orange bell pepper, sliced into rings
- 4 tomatoes, sliced into rounds
- ¼ cup blue cheese, crumbled

Instructions:
1. Mix the vinegar, olive oil, mustard, basil, chives, sugar and pepper in a bowl.
2. Arrange the tomatoes and pepper rings in a serving plate.
3. Sprinkle the crumbled blue cheese on top.
4. Drizzle with the dressing.
5. Chill in the refrigerator for 1 hour before serving.

Nutrition: Calories 116 Fat 7 g Saturated fat 2 g - Carbohydrates 11 g Fiber 2 g Protein 3 g

Cucumber Tomato Chopped Salad

Preparation Time: 15 minutes
Cooking Time: 0 minute
Servings: 6

Ingredients:
- ½ cup light mayonnaise
- 1 tablespoon lemon juice
- 1 tablespoon fresh dill, chopped
- 1 tablespoon chives, chopped
- ½ cup feta cheese, crumbled
- Salt and pepper to taste
- 1 red onion, chopped
- 1 cucumber, diced
- 1 radish, diced
- 3 tomatoes, diced
- Chives, chopped

Directions:
1. Combine the mayo, lemon juice, fresh dill, chives, feta cheese, salt and pepper in a bowl.
2. Mix well.
3. Stir in the onion, cucumber, radish and tomatoes.
4. Coat evenly.
5. Garnish with the chopped chives.

Nutrition: Calories 187 Fat 16.7 g Saturated fat 4.1 g Carbohydrates 6.7 g Fiber 2 g Protein 3.3 g

GRAINS

Chickpea and Spinach Cutlets

Preparation Time: 10 minutes
Cooking Time: 30 minutes
Servings: 12

Ingredients:
- 1 Red Bell Pepper
- 19 oz. Chickpeas, Rinsed & Drained
- 1 c. ground Almonds
- 2 tsps. Dijon Mustard
- 1 tsp. Oregano
- ½ tsp. Sage
- 1 c. Spinach, Fresh
- 1½ c. Rolled Oats
- 1 Clove Garlic, Pressed
- ½ Lemon, Juiced
- 2 tsps. Maple Syrup, Pure

Directions:
1. Get out a baking sheet. Line it with parchment paper.
2. Cut your red pepper in half and then take the seeds out. Place it on your baking sheet, and roast in the oven while you prepare your other ingredients.
3. Process your chickpeas, almonds, mustard, and maple syrup together in a food processor.
4. Add in your lemon juice, oregano, sage, garlic, and spinach, processing again. Make sure it's combined, but don't puree it.
5. Once your red bell pepper is softened, which should roughly take ten minutes, add this to the processor as well. Add in your oats, mixing well.
6. Form twelve patties, cooking in the oven for a half hour. They should be browned.

Nutrition: Calories: 200, Protein: 8 g, Fat: 11g, Carbs: 21 g

Savory Spanish Rice

Preparation Time: 5 minutes
Cooking Time: 5 hours
Servings: 10

Ingredients:
- 1 c. long grain rice, uncooked
- ½ c. green bell pepper, chopped
- 14 oz. diced tomatoes
- ½ c. chopped white onion
- 1 tsp. minced garlic
- ½ tsp. salt
- 1 tsp. red chili powder
- 1 tsp. ground cumin
- 4 oz. tomato puree
- 8 fl. oz. water

Directions:
1. Grease a 6-quarts slow cooker with a non-stick cooking spray and add all the ingredients into it.
2. Stir properly and cover the top.
3. Plug in the slow cooker; adjust the cooking time to 5 hours, and cook on high or until the rice absorbs all the liquid.

Nutrition: Calories:210 Cal, Carbs:11g, Protein:12g, Fats:10g.

Raw Noodles with Avocado 'N Nuts

Preparation Time: 5 minutes
Cooking Time: 10 minutes
Servings: 2

Ingredients:
- 1 zucchini
- 1½ c. basil
- 1/3 c. water
- 5 tbsps. pine nuts
- 2 tbsps. lemon juice
- 1 avocado, peeled, pitted, sliced
- Optional: 2 tbsps. olive oil
- 6 yellow cherry tomatoes, halved
- Optional: 6 red cherry tomatoes, halved
- Sea salt and black pepper

Directions:
1. Add the basil, water, nuts, lemon juice, avocado slices, optional olive oil (if desired), salt, and pepper to a blender.
2. Blend the ingredients into a smooth mixture. Season with more pepper and salt and blend again.
3. Divide the sauce and the zucchini noodles between two medium-sized bowls for serving, and combine in each.
4. Top the mixtures with the halved yellow cherry tomatoes, and the optional red cherry tomatoes (if desired);

Nutrition: Calories 317, Carbs 7.4 g, Fats 28.1 g, Protein 7.2 g

LEGUMES

Indian Chana Masala

Preparation Time: 10 minutes
Cooking Time: 10 minutes
Servings: 4

Ingredients:

- 1 cup tomatoes, pureed
- 1 Kashmiri chile pepper, chopped
- 1 large shallot, chopped
- 1 teaspoon fresh ginger, peeled and grated
- 4 tablespoons olive oil
- 2 cloves garlic, minced
- 1 teaspoon coriander seeds
- 1 teaspoon garam masala
- 1/2 teaspoon turmeric powder
- Sea salt and ground black pepper, to taste
- 1/2 cup vegetable broth
- 16 ounces canned chickpeas
- 1 tablespoon fresh lime juice

Directions

1. In your blender or food processor, blend the tomatoes, Kashmiri chile pepper, shallot and ginger into a paste.
2. In a saucepan, heat the olive oil over medium heat.
3. Once hot, cook the prepared paste and garlic for about 2 minutes.
4. Add in the remaining spices, broth and chickpeas.
5. Turn the heat to a simmer. Continue to simmer for 8 minutes more or until cooked through.
6. Remove from the heat. Drizzle fresh lime juice over the top of each serving. Bon appétit!

Nutrition: Calories: 305; Fat: 17.1g; Carbs: 30.1g; Protein: 9.4g

BREAD & PIZZA

Jalapeno Cheese Bread

Preparation Time: 10 Minutes
Cooking Time: 60 Minutes
Servings: 8

Ingredients:
- Egg – 1
- Flour – 2 cups
- Jalapeno pepper – 1, minced
- Cheddar cheese – 1 1/4 cups, shredded

- Butter – 1/4 cup, melted
- Milk – 1/4 cup
- Yogurt – 3/4 cup
- Sugar – 2 tablespoons.
- Baking soda – 1/2 teaspoon.
- Baking powder– 1 1/2 teaspoon.
- Salt – 1/2 teaspoon.

Directions:

1. Preheat the oven to 350 F. In a bowl, mix together flour, sugar, baking soda, baking powder, and salt.
2. In a separate bowl, whisk together egg, milk, butter, and yogurt. Add egg mixture into the flour mixture and mix until well combined.
3. Stir in jalapeno, and shredded cheese. Pour batter into the parchment-lined 9.5-inch baking tin and bake for 1 hour.
4. Allow to cool for 10-15 minutes. Slice and serve.

Nutrition: Calories 276, Carbs 29.6g, Fat 12.9g, Protein 9.9g

SOUP AND STEW

Tomato Gazpacho

Preparation Time: 30 minutes
Cooking Time: 55 minutes
Servings: 6

Ingredients:
- 2 Tablespoons + 1 Teaspoon Red Wine Vinegar, Divided
- ½ Teaspoon Pepper
- 1 Teaspoon Sea Salt
- 1 Avocado,
- ¼ Cup Basil, Fresh & Chopped
- 3 Tablespoons + 2 Teaspoons Olive Oil, Divided

- 1 Clove Garlic, crushed
- 1 Red Bell Pepper, Sliced & Seeded
- 1 Cucumber, Chunked
- 2 ½ lbs. Large Tomatoes, Cored & Chopped

Directions:

1. Place half of your cucumber, bell pepper, and ¼ cup of each tomato in a bowl, covering. Set it in the fried.
2. Puree your remaining tomatoes, cucumber and bell pepper with garlic, three tablespoons oil, two tablespoons of vinegar, sea salt and black pepper into a blender, blending until smooth. Transfer it to a bowl, and chill for two hours.
3. Chop the avocado, adding it to your chopped vegetables, adding your remaining oil, vinegar, salt, pepper and basil.
4. Ladle your tomato puree mixture into bowls, and serve with chopped vegetables as a salad.
5. Interesting Facts:
6. Avocados themselves are ranked within the top five of the healthiest foods on the planet, so you know that the oil produced from them is too. It is loaded with healthy fats and essential fatty acids.
7. Like race bran oil it is perfect to cook with as well!
8. Bonus: Helps in the prevention of diabetes and lowers cholesterol levels.

Nutrition: Calories 201 Protein 23g Fat 4 Carbs 2

Tomato Pumpkin Soup

Preparation Time: 25 minutes
Cooking Time: 25 minutes
Servings: 4

Ingredients:

- 2 cups pumpkin, diced
- 1/2 cup tomato, chopped
- 1/2 cup onion, chopped
- 1 1/2 tsp curry powder

- 1/2 tsp paprika
- 2 cups vegetable stock
- 1 tsp olive oil
- 1/2 tsp garlic, minced

Directions:

1. In a saucepan, add oil, garlic, and onion and sauté for 3 minutes over medium heat.
2. Add remaining ingredients into the saucepan and bring to boil.
3. Reduce heat and cover and simmer for 10 minutes.
4. Puree the soup using a blender until smooth.
5. Stir well and serve warm.

Nutrition: Calories: 340 Protein: 50 g Carbohydrate: 14 g Fat: 10g

SAUCE, DRESSINGS & DIP

Avocado Hummus

Preparation time: 5 minutes

Cooking time: 5 minutes
Servings: 6

Ingredients:

- 1 tablespoon. cilantro, finely chopped
- 1/8 t. cumin
- 1 clove garlic
- 3 tablespoons. lime juice
- 1 1/2 tablespoon. of the following:
- Tahini
- Olive oil
- 2 avocados, medium cored & peeled
- 15 oz. chickpeas, drained
- Salt and pepper to taste

Directions:

1. In a food processor, add garlic, lime juice, tahini, olive oil, chickpeas, and pulse until combined.
2. Add cumin and avocados and blend until smooth consistency approximately 2 minutes.
3. Add salt and pepper to taste.

Nutrition: Calories: 310 Carbohydrates: 26 g Proteins: 8 g Fats: 20 g

Guacamole with Tomato

Preparation time: 5 minutes
Cooking time: 5 minutes
Servings: 6

Ingredients:

- 3 tablespoons of the following:
- Tomato, diced
- Onion, diced
- 2 tablespoons of the following:
- Cilantro, chopped
- Jalapeno juice
- 1/4 t. garlic powder
- 1/2 t. salt

- 1/2 lime, squeezed
- 2 big avocados
- 1 jalapeno, diced

Directions:

1. Using a molcajete, crush the diced jalapenos until soft.
2. Add the avocados to the molcajete.
3. Squeeze the lime juice from ½ of the lime on top of the avocados.
4. Add the jalapeno juice, garlic, and salt and mix until smooth.
5. Once smooth, add in the onion, cilantro, and tomato and stir to incorporate.

Nutrition: Calories: 127 Carbohydrates: 9.3 g Proteins: 2.4 g Fats: 10.2 g

APPETIZER

Scrumptious Ginger Cookies

Preparation time: 15 minutes
Cooking time: 10 minutes
Servings: 12
Ingredients:

- 1 tsp ground cinnamon
- 1 large organic egg
- 1/2 tbsp ground ginger
- 1/4 tsp sea salt
- 3/4 cup coconut flour
- 3/4 cup unsalted butter (softened)
- 3/4 cup powdered brown sugar erythritol
- 1 1/2 cups almond flour

Directions:

1. Prepare two baking sheets lined using parchment paper and preheat oven to 350oF. In a bowl, whisk well salt, cinnamon, ginger, coconut flour, and almond flour.
2. Add egg and beat well to mix. Knead until you form a dough. Scoop into balls. Roll in powdered erythritol.
3. Place in prepared baking sheet two inches apart. Flatten each cookie and bake until golden brown, around 9 minutes.

Nutrition: Calories: 190 Protein: 3.5g Carbs: 5.5g Fat: 16.0g

Cinnamon Muffins

Preparation time: 15 minutes
Cooking time: 15 minutes
Servings: 12

Ingredients:
- 1 tbsp cinnamon
- 1 tsp baking powder
- 1/2 cup almond flour
- 1/2 cup coconut oil
- 1/2 cup almond butter
- 1/2 cup pumpkin puree
- 2 scoops vanilla protein powder
- Glaze Ingredients:
- 1 tbsp granulated sweetener of choice
- 2 tsp lemon juice
- 1/4 cup coconut butter
- 1/4 cup milk of choice

Directions:
1. Line 12 muffin tins with muffin liners and preheat oven to 350oF. Whisk well cinnamon, baking powder, and protein powder in a medium bowl.

2. Whisk in coconut oil, almond butter, and pumpkin puree. Mix well. Evenly divide into prepared muffin tins.

3. Bake in the oven for 13 minutes or until cooked through. Move it to a wire rack and let it cool. Meanwhile, mix all glaze ingredients in a small bowl and drizzle over cooled muffin.

Nutrition: Calories: 112Protein: 5.0gCarbs: 3.0gFat: 9.0g

Vegan Avocado & Spinach Dip

Preparation time: 15 minutes
Cooking time: 0 minutes
Servings: 12

Ingredients:
- 1 garlic clove crushed
- 1 tbsp Extra virgin avocado oil
- 1 tablespoon lime juice
- 1/2 cup fresh spinach leaves in boiling water within 2 minutes, squeezed, drained
- 1/2 teaspoon sea salt
- 1/4 cup fresh coriander chopped
- 2 large ripe avocados about 2 cups of mashed avocado
- 3 tablespoon Extra Virgin Avocado Oil
- 3/4 cup dairy free coconut yogurt

Directions:
1. With paper towel, pat dry blanched spinach leaves. In a blender or food processor, puree pepper, salt, avocado oil, lime juice, coconut yogurt, coriander, crushed garlic, and ripe avocado.
2. Transfer to a bowl and whisk in spinach leaves. Serve and enjoy.

Nutrition: Calories: 91Protein: 1.1gCarbs: 3.1gFat: 8.8g

SMOOTHIES AND JUICES

Easy and Fresh Mango Madness

Preparation Time: 5 minutes
Cooking Time: 0 minutes
Servings: 4
Ingredients:
- 1 cup chopped mango
- 1 cup chopped peach
- 1 banana
- 1 cup strawberries
- 1 carrot, peeled and chopped
- 1 cup water

Directions:

1. Put all the ingredients in a food processor, then blitz until glossy and smooth.
2. Serve immediately or chill in the refrigerator for an hour before serving.

Nutrition: calories: 376 fat: 22.0gcarbs: 19.0g fiber: 14.0g protein: 5.0g

Simple Date Shake

Preparation Time: 10 minutes
Cooking Time: 0 minutes
Servings: 2

Ingredients:
- 5 Medjool dates, pitted, soaked in boiling water for 5 minutes
- ¾ cup unsweetened coconut milk
  - teaspoon vanilla extract
- ½ teaspoon fresh lemon juice
- ¼ teaspoon sea salt, optional
- 1½ cups ice

Directions:
1. Put all the ingredients in a food processor, then blitz until it has a milkshake and smooth texture.
2. Serve immediately.

Nutrition: calories: 380 fat: 21.6gcarbs: 50.3gfiber: 6.0gprotein: 3.2g

DESSETRS

Almond-Date Energy Bites

Preparation time: 25 minutes
Cooking time: 0 minutes
Servings: 24

Ingredients:
- cup dates, pitted
- cup unsweetened shredded coconut
- ¼ cup chia seeds
- ¾ cup ground almonds
- ¼ cup cocoa nibs, or non-dairy chocolate chips

Directions:
1. Purée everything in a food processor until crumbly and sticking together, pushing down the sides whenever necessary to keep it blending.

2. Form the mix into 24 balls and place them on a baking sheet lined with parchment or waxed paper.
3. Put in the fridge to set for about 15 minutes.

Nutrition: Calories: 152Fat: 11gCarbs: 13gProtein: 3g

Coconut and Almond Truffles

Preparation time: 15 minutes
Cooking time: 0 minutes
Servings: 8
Ingredients:
- cup pitted dates
- cup almonds
- ½ cup sweetened cocoa powder, plus extra for coating
- ½ cup unsweetened shredded coconut
- ¼ cup pure maple syrup
- teaspoon vanilla extract
- 1 teaspoon almond extract
- ¼ teaspoon sea salt

Directions:
1. In the bowl of a food processor, combine all the ingredients and process until smooth. Chill the mixture for about 1 hour.
2. Roll the batter into balls then roll it in cocoa powder to coat.
3. Serve immediately or keep chilled until ready to serve.

Nutrition: Calories: 74 Carbs: 8g Fat: 4g Protein: 1g

Chocolate Macaroons

Preparation time: 15 minutes
Cooking time: 15 minutes
Servings: 8

Ingredients:
- cup unsweetened shredded coconut

- tablespoons cocoa powder
- 2/3 cup coconut milk
- ¼ cup agave
- pinch of sea salt

Directions:

1. Preheat the oven to 350°F. Line a baking sheet with parchment paper.
2. In a medium saucepan, cook all the fixings over-medium-high heat until a firm dough is formed.
3. Scoop the dough into balls and place on the baking sheet.
4. Bake for 15 minutes, remove from the oven, and let cool on the baking sheet. Serve cooled macaroons.

Nutrition: Calories: 141 Carbs: 1g Fat: 8g Protein: 1g

Chocolate Pudding

Preparation time: 5 minutes
Cooking time: 0 minutes
Servings: 1

Ingredients:

- banana
- to 4 tablespoons nondairy milk
- tablespoons unsweetened cocoa powder
- 2 tablespoons sugar (optional)
- ½ ripe avocado or 1 cup silken tofu (optional)

Directions:

1. In a small blender, combine the banana, milk, cocoa powder, sugar (if using), and avocado (if using).
2. Purée until smooth.
3. Alternatively, in a small bowl, mash the banana very well, and stir in the remaining ingredients.

Nutrition: Calories: 244Protein: 4gFat: 3gCarbohydrates: 59g

Lime and Watermelon Granita

Preparation time: 6 hours & 15 minutes
Cooking time: 0 minutes
Servings: 4

Ingredients:
- 8 cups seedless watermelon chunks
- juice of 2 limes, or 2 tablespoons prepared lime juice
- ½ cup sugar
- strips of lime zest, for garnish

Directions:
1. Mix the watermelon, lime juice, plus sugar in a blender or food processor and process until smooth.
2. After processing, stir well to combine both batches.
3. Pour the mixture into a 9-by-13-inch glass dish.
4. Freeze for 2 to 3 hours.
5. Remove then use a fork to scrape the top layer of ice.
6. Leave the shaved ice on top and return to the freezer.
7. In another hour, remove from the freezer and repeat. Do this a few more times until all the ice is scraped up.
8. Serve frozen, garnished with strips of lime zest.

Nutrition: Calories: 70 Carbs: 18g Fat: 0g Protein: 1g

Mint Chocolate Fat Bombs

Preparation time: 15 minutes
Cooking time: 0 minutes
Servings: 6

Ingredients:
- 2/3 cup coconut oil, melted
- tablespoon erythritol, granulated

- ¼ teaspoon peppermint extract
- tablespoons unsweetened cocoa powder

Directions:
1. Mix the coconut oil, erythritol, and peppermint extract in a small mixing bowl.
2. Use a silicone mold and fill six of the cups only halfway with the mixture.
3. Place the mold in the refrigerator for 5 minutes.
4. Add the cocoa powder to the remaining mixture and stir well.
5. Pour a cocoa layer on top of each peppermint layer and place the mold back in the refrigerator until set.
6. Use a butter knife to remove the bombs from the mold (they should just pop right out) and place them in a resealable freezer bag.
7. Store in the refrigerator or freezer.

Nutrition: Calories: 229 Fat: 25g Protein: 0g Carbs: 1g

Printed in Great Britain
by Amazon